pocket superdate

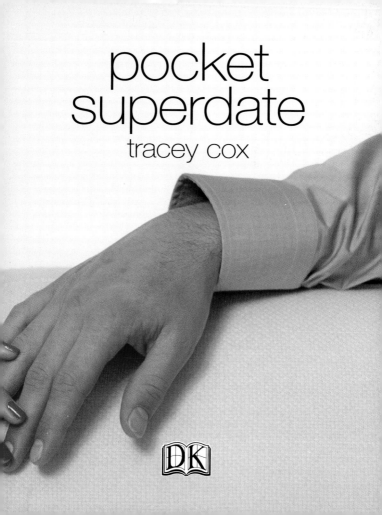

pocket
superdate

tracey cox

DK

LONDON, NEW YORK, MUNICH,
MELBOURNE, DELHI

Senior Art Editor Nicola Rodway
Senior Editor Peter Jones
Editor Elizabeth Watson
Executive Managing Editor Adèle Hayward
Managing Art Editor Karla Jennings
DTP Designer Traci Salter
Production Controller Luca Frassinetti
Art Director Peter Luff
Publishing Director Corinne Roberts

**Produced for DK by
Dawn Bates and Emma Forge.**

Photography by Russell Sadur

First published in Great Britain in 2006
by Dorling Kindersley Limited,
80 Strand, London WC2R 0RL

A Penguin Company

2 4 6 8 10 9 7 5 3 1

A CIP catalogue record for this book is
available from the British Library.

ISBN-13: 978-1-4053-1681-1
ISBN-10: 1-4053-1681-0

Printed and bound in Singapore
by Star Standard

see our complete catalogue at
www.dk.com

Contents

Introduction

This is a handy, take-anywhere pocket-size version of my original book, *superdate*. It's a book about body language and how it can help you be more successful in relationships. It's primarily aimed at singles looking for love, but quite frankly it's useful to anyone who wants to get on better with people in any situation.

As with all my books, this one is written from a heterosexual point of view but it applies equally to gay or lesbian relationships. My apologies (again), for not covering the myriad of partnerships out there – it was done purely for simplicity's sake. I toyed with the idea of a separate chapter on gay and lesbian body language but I honestly don't think it's markedly different from straights. While some gay men like to adopt more feminine gestures and some lesbians acquire more masculine traits, it's my observation that most continue to send the same signals to attract a partner as straights do. Only difference being the partner you're aiming the signals at, happens to be the same sex.

The prime purpose of *pocket superdate* is to turn you into one. What you might find odd, given the title, is a distinct lack of chapters on pick-up-lines, what to wear, and where to go. The usual stuff you find in dating books is missing because while those things are important, what's crucial to your attractiveness and chances of finding a deliciously decadent dalliance is the ability to send and receive clear signals.

Body language is the focus of *pocket superdate* – for good reason. Most relationships are formed or dismissed within the first

The **prime purpose of *superdate*** is to turn you into one.

five minutes of meeting. We rely mainly on body language to decide who we like and who we don't because (boring buggers that we are) most initial conversations centre around small talk and trivia. With no real verbal clues of character, we're forced to instead depend on deciphering unspoken signals. There never was a truer saying than actions speak louder than words!

To get the most from this book, it's best to read it on two levels: to check your own body language ("Am I sending clear signals?") and to decode the subliminal signals people send you, so you can make quick, informed choices about potential partners based on the little information and little time that's usually available. Once

It is entirely possible to make someone **fall in love with you.**

you've done that and are skipping off into the sunset/slamming the door of the nearest bedroom with someone lovely, the book is useful to help constantly monitor your new relationship, so both of you end up happy ever after.

The Rule of Four and why it's crucially important: Without "The Rule of Four", you'll be jumping to all sorts of bizarre conclusions as you're trying to read potential partners. The basic premise is this: don't ever judge on one thing alone. Think of each clue, signal, or gesture someone sends you as a word in a sentence. While one word alone can make sense ("help"), it can also completely change meaning when put into context ("you just can't get good help these days"). In order to get the full picture, you need to look for other "words" to build a sentence i.e. look for "clusters" of body language. Sitting with your arms crossed often means you're feeling huffy and defensive. But it can also mean it's bloody freezing or you're conscious of your tummy after scoffing a gigantic bag of crisps! The Rule of Four stops you jumping to silly conclusions because it insists you always look for at least four body language signals, all happening simultaneously and all pointing to the same conclusion, before making a judgement call. Got it? Great! Now let's get started...

the**meeting**

Love at first sight might not be reliable or even long-lasting but instant attraction isn't just a figment of a hopeful imagination.

Simply lock eyes with someone you're hugely attracted to and your heart rate quickens and blood pressure soars. We communicate more with our eyes than any other body part. Hide your eyes and you hide your emotions. Narrowed eyes scream suspicion, a raised brow poses a question, eyes brimming with tears radiate excitement or sorrow – our eyes and the muscles around them clearly communicate what emotion we're feeling. Which is why it's almost impossible to flirt or fall in love without eye contact – zero eye communication usually means zero connection.

Just in case it isn't sinking in, let me put this even more clearly because if you want to pull a partner, it's crucial you get this bit right! Spend time studying the eye-scanning sequence on the next two pages – particularly if you're a guy. Reading the signs correctly when you first meet really helps you sort out who wants you and who doesn't!

The eye scan

When it comes to sizing each other up, men and women differ. Men tend to scan from the feet up, while women tend to scan from the face down.

Where we look Interested men and women usually send three sidelong glances. The first from men starts at the feet and moves up the body to the face – scanning in order of what they think is important! Women start at the eyes and then look down, the order of what's most important to them.

Count the looks The first look we get is to see if we're worth looking at. You'll get a second look if they liked what they saw (to confirm the first), and a third if they're so impressed they're considering talking to you.

▼ **her eye** scan

The four-second scan Pass this test and they'll keep glancing your way to evaluate how open you are to being approached. We look at strangers or uninteresting people for three seconds or less. If someone's tossing you continual four-second gazes, it's a definite sign they're keen.

How they break the gaze Now listen up, this is the interesting bit… how a woman breaks eye contact is critical. If she moves her eyes to the side, continuing to look around the room, hailing a cab won't be necessary. She's still searching for better. If her eyes drop straight to the floor before looking back up again to meet yours within 30 seconds to a minute, you've hit gold. Downcast eyes followed by a preening gesture or hair-tossing and she definitely likes what she sees. So far, so good!

his eye scan

Spot who's single

So how do you spot who's single in a group – and make it clear that you are single too?

A green light from her Her shoulders are pulled back to thrust her breasts forward. (A good move – in the days when people hitched lifts, one study found a woman hitching could double the number of lifts she was offered by adding two inches of padding to her bra!) Putting a hand on the back of a hip emphasizes a tiny waist. Her eyes may also narrow – this sharpens focus and allows her to examine you more carefully. Not to mention making her look damn sexy!

A green light from him He'll stand with hands on hips, jacket pushed back, feet apart. He'll also perform a chest thrust to make himself look dominant. Both men and women swell and shrink accordingly to signal importance, fear, and desired attractiveness.

You or they do a double take You look, turn away, then when the impact of what you've seen sinks in, turn back immediately. Dished up with a cheeky smile ("My God! How gorgeous are you!") it's dynamite! Shyer types can try locking eyes for a fraction of a second and looking straight to the floor, before casting a swift glance over one shoulder.

Friends or lovers? So how can you tell if two people together are lovers or friends? In-love couples tilt their heads towards each other; in-lust lovers, mesh the lower part of their bodies. Attached couples usually let the other know what they're up to, through a touch, a look, or words. When they talk, they'll look at their partner often.

Tempting trio
A smile, direct eye contact, and head tilted to the side. There's also space between her and her friend – she's single alright!

Body turned towards you Even if she weren't making direct eye contact, turning her torso your way is a subconscious sexual body display.

Open formation
A foot pointed towards you says you're welcome to join us and make it a threesome.

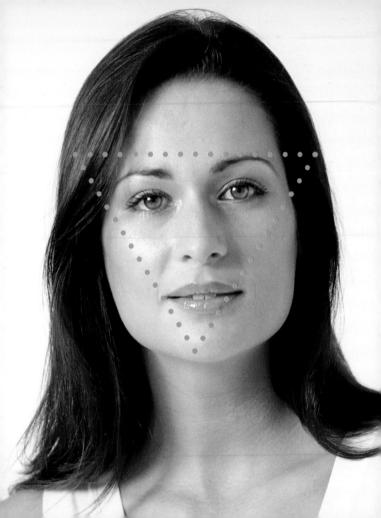

The flirting triangle

When looking at strangers, we look from eye to eye, dipping slightly across the nose to make a tiny triangle. With friends, the triangle widens as eyes drop to include the nose and mouth. When looking at longed-for lovers, it broadens further to include even better bits like the breasts and genitals, hence the term "flirting triangle".

> # We fall in love with large pupils without ever really knowing why.

Pupil size When lovers stare into each other's eyes, they're unconsciously checking the degree of pupil dilation. Bottomless, black pits instinctively reassure us all is well, pinprick pupils make us squirm for good reason – pupils enlarge when we like what we see. In one experiment, men were shown two pictures of an attractive girl, both identical except one set was doctored to make the pupils larger. Almost all judged the girl with bigger pupils more attractive, though none could say why. It almost certainly means that the men were attracted to the girl that they felt liked them. We like to be liked!

Giveaway signs If you want to know if someone fancies you, look for their eyebrows rising and falling. It's called an eyebrow flash – watch for it in the first 60 seconds of meeting.

Reading feet

1

On target

You can tell what's happening with this couple, just by looking at their feet. The transition from attracted strangers to flirtatious friends is clearly communicated purely through the position of their feet. To begin with, his feet point squarely at his target, showing obvious (and, given he doesn't shift position, unwavering) interest in her. Initially she's not sure. One leg crosses over the other, meaning she's slightly defensive, but the front foot is angled to point in his direction, so it's still looking promising.

2

Mirroring

She uncrosses her legs and moves closer, mirroring his feet position – a clear sign they're getting on well. Feet are an incredibly reliable indicator of our true feelings because they're the body part farthest from the face. Few notice or think to control their legs or feet. This puts them extremely high on the believability scale. Walk into a meeting and you'll notice all feet usually point to the boss. Watch men at a party: their torsos might dutifully turn towards their partner but their feet will often point towards another pretty girl.

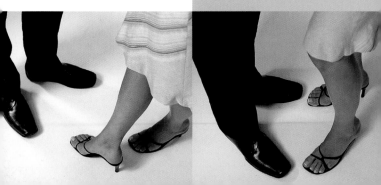

3
Close up

The symbolism of her foot between his legs suggests strong sexual interest – both are subliminally imitating what might happen later sexually. The icing on the cake would be if she kicked her shoes off when they sat down. Bare feet mean bed because taking your shoes off is the first stage of stripping. Our feet aren't the only things we point with, by the way. Both men and women put their hands on their hips, fingers splayed and pointing downwards to show off another obvious good bit!

Tips and tricks

● The lighter the step, the lighter the heart. Happy people tend to "bounce" and lift their feet high, as though they were made of air, rather than lead.

● If you're female, every time you place a foot forward, put it dead centre instead of to the side. "Toeing the line" is an old catwalk trick that forces a wiggle.

● Stand with your feet a few inches apart rather than your heels snapped together. You'll feel more stable and grounded and as a result appear more open and approachable to people.

We point with our feet to what we want.

Don't bother

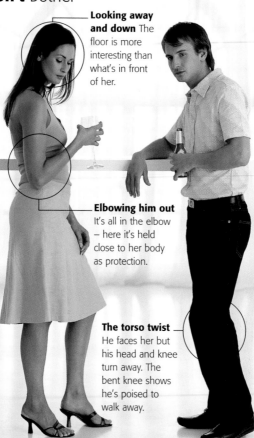

Looking away and down The floor is more interesting than what's in front of her.

Elbowing him out It's all in the elbow – here it's held close to her body as protection.

The torso twist He faces her but his head and knee turn away. The bent knee shows he's poised to walk away.

Both **interested**

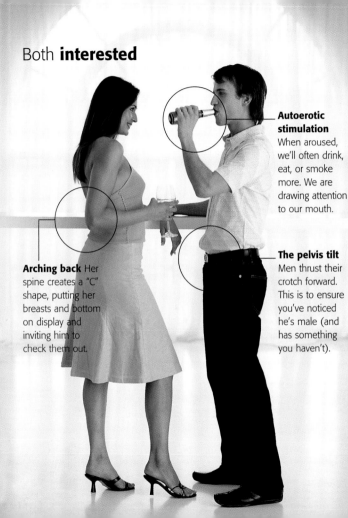

Autoerotic stimulation
When aroused, we'll often drink, eat, or smoke more. We are drawing attention to our mouth.

Arching back Her spine creates a "C" shape, putting her breasts and bottom on display and inviting him to check them out.

The pelvis tilt
Men thrust their crotch forward. This is to ensure you've noticed he's male (and has something you haven't).

Body blocks

Purse held as shield

When we feel vulnerable, our natural instinct is to hide behind a barrier. We feel safer when we're behind a shield. As children we'd run and hide under Mum's skirt or beneath the nearest table when we felt threatened. As adults, our instincts still tell us to do the same thing but, sadly, such behaviour is not socially acceptable. Instead, we find ways to erect what are more acceptable barriers: we'll place a chair or table in front of us or hold a purse, handbag, book, or drink high up, near to our chest, which gives us the illusion of safety.

Fiddling with shirt cuff

The image below shows a disguised arm-cross – he's trying to conceal that he's feeling uncertain by fiddling with his cufflinks. People who realize the implications of crossing their arms sneakily achieve the feeling of security through other means. An arm swings across the body but instead of gripping the other arm, the hand fiddles with a cufflink, bracelet, or pulls down a sleeve. Another disguised arm barrier often used? Holding our drink with both hands. It's not like we need two hands to hold a glass, is it now?

Partial arm barrier

Crossing arms tightly across the chest is an instinctive, primitive attempt to protect vital organs: the heart and lungs. It's also an obvious sign you're nervous or defensive. Holding one arm across the body is slightly more subtle and gets the same result; holding hands with yourself, in front of your body, is another version. Both sexes use arm barriers but women fold their arms much lower on the body. The reason? Breasts! An alternative is grounding yourself. You'll get the same comfort by lightly leaning against a wall or piece of furniture.

Fighting fair

Watch for the following when you're arguing with someone:

- If you're about to have a heavy discussion and their arms are crossed before you talk, you've got your work cut out: they've already decided to respond negatively. It's essential they uncross them, so hand them something like a drink.
- If their hand is gripping their arm, they're determined to hang on to their bad mood or attitude – settle in for the long haul!
- If their arms are crossed and both hands are hidden beneath their arms they're hiding their tight fists. This means they're *really* angry!

Even **one arm held across the body** makes us look defensive.

We can **sense someone watching us even** with our backs turned.

Tracey's top tips

Take the 60-second compatibility test

Chat to someone for ten minutes, then secretly ask yourself the following questions (don't think too much about the answers): Would you like to kiss this person? Would they get on with your best friend? Would you like to have their child? Would you like to be more like this person? Your knee-jerk reaction will reveal more than you think.

Watch the way they fondle the furniture

Sometimes, we try to make contact through an intermediate object. The person who grabs hold of the back of the chair you're sitting on, or puts an arm along the back of the sofa behind you, is trying to get close. The message: they're too scared to touch you or they're testing to see what would happen if they did.

Don't make classic mistakes

Make too much eye contact and you'll be seen as superior, threatening, or adoring. Too little sends shy, insincere, or not-interested signals. Lowering your eyes briefly is a great flirting move but leave them down there and you'll appear submissive. If someone avoids looking at you, don't assume it means lack of interest. You could be discussing a difficult subject or they might be in awe of you.

Do believe body language over words

If there's a choice, people will nearly always believe the body. "I hate you," said with a cheeky smile, tipped chin, and sexy smile actually means the opposite. "I don't fancy her" doesn't hold much weight if the person casts long, frequent glances at the girl in question.

2

the**chat-up**

What's the first thing you do when someone gorgeous walks in the room? Make sure you look your best of course! It's called preening or grooming – "straightening ourselves out".

Men smooth or ruffle their hair, straighten their tie, tweak their jackets, pull up sagging socks, and brush specks from their clothes. A classic male preening sign is surreptitiously licking a finger and smoothing an unruly eyebrow into place.

Women check their hair with their hands, smooth skirts to show off their hips – and more often than not, disappear to the bathroom to do a full mirror check and lipstick touch-up. It's all part of the mating ritual.

Once we think we look OK, we're ready to move into "illuminations" – me-Tarzan, you-Jane gestures that highlight the physical difference between the sexes. Sticking your breasts out, for instance, reminds him he doesn't have any. Standing with legs apart and crotch thrust forwards does the same for her.

The twist of a wrist

Guys, perhaps her hands and arms are going to be the last part of her body you focus on, but it's worth paying attention to her wrists and palms because they can tell you all you need to know.

Women, almost predictably, flash their wrist at someone they're attracted to – it's such a clichéd feminine response that wrist-flashing often has a starring role in a drag queen's repertoire of exaggerated girly gestures. Watch while a woman fiddles with her hair, an earring, or smokes a cigarette, and look to see if the wrist is turned to face you, palm exposed. Great news if it is. Open palms nearly always mean good things – which is why a mere flick of the wrist can change the mood and message instantly.

> By flashing her wrist she's saying, **'I won't fight you. Go ahead, chat me up.'**

If the palms represent honesty and openness, by showing you the back of her hand she's saying the opposite: bugger off. It means she'd prefer it if you backed off big time – you're coming way too close. If, when seated opposite you, she's flipped her hand and rested her chin on it, she has effectively hung a neon sign saying, "Bored" so take the hint!

Superior steepling

Do you want to give the impression you know exactly what you're talking about? Put your fingertips together, palms facing, and make a church steeple. It's called "steepling" (no, really) and it'll be the best thing you ever did with your fingers, or the worst. If you're on the receiving end of someone who is steepling, it probably means they think they're superior to you.

People tend to steeple up when talking and down *(bottom left)* when listening. We make a moderate steeple *(bottom right)* when we think we know more than the person speaking. The higher the steeple,

the more arrogant you risk appearing, which is why women (more fearful of looking arrogant) tend to favour the lowered variety.

How your steeple is interpreted depends on accompanying body language and how you hold your hands while steepling. If you're an authority on something, a high steeple is a good move – it shows you're confident and know your stuff. Tilt your head back and "look down your nose", however, and you'll transform into a pompous twit.

A "disguised steeple" is when someone joins their fingers and covers their mouth. It is often a sign that they know better than the person they're with and are trying to stop themselves from saying so.

Watch how she touches her throat

Women usually touch their throat for two different reasons: when they're feeling vulnerable or flirty.

• **Not good:** her hand winds around her throat or covers it and stays in that position. You may have offended her physically or emotionally and "gone for the jugular" – her hand flies into position literally to protect it by forming a barrier. The message to you is: stop whatever it is you're doing or talking about, backtrack, and reassure her.

• **Good:** stroking her throat, neck, or upper chest sends an erotic signal. Our throats and necks are "lovers-only" zones – no-one else touches us there. If it's combined with a neck-arch, the signal is even more potent – exposing her throat is a hint she's starting to trust you.

Leg crossed high on thigh The higher she crosses her legs, the more sexual the signal and the more she fancies you. Add direct eye contact, a smile, and one hand leading your eyes to her genital area, and there's a flashing green light.

Open toe shoes Serious, sensible girls tend not to wear high, strappy sandals. If the shoes are frivolous – designed to look good, not good for comfort – she's likely to be out to have a fun time (and keen to meet you!).

Legging it

We cross our arms instinctively to protect our heart and vital organs (and all the emotions associated with them), we cross our legs to shield our genitals (ditto). But while crossed arms nearly always have a negative connotation, women often cross their legs to show them off, to look "ladylike" or sexy. Because legs are in the bottom half of the body and farther away from our face and general vision, they're quite a reliable indicator of our true feelings.

Sitting with legs apart Confident men often sit this way but it's rare for a women to sit with legs apart, even if they're covered by jeans or trousers. In a skirt, she'd almost never assume this pose (unless you're already lovers and she's teasing you). Any woman who plants her legs wide open literally wears the pants. She's powerful and challenging. Not a good bet if you're looking for someone to bake cookies.

Sitting with legs tightly crossed Men do it when they're feeling defensive. "Proper" girls do it to form an invisible chastity belt. Trouble is, the more fuss you make covering up your sexual parts, the more it draws other people's attention to them. Yanking down a too short skirt only highlights the length!

Walking on tiptoe If she's on the beach, by a pool, or anywhere where women take their shoes off, whether or not she rises on her tiptoes is highly significant. If attractive men are around, she will. Being on her tiptoes makes her legs look longer, her body slimmer, and her look more feminine.

How are you doing so far?

So now I've given you a taster, let's stop and take stock, find out if you're doing okay, and remind you why you're doing it. Just in case you were naughty and skipped the introduction, let's remind ourselves what we're trying to do here.

To qualify as a "superdate", you need to:
a) attract the person you want
b) seduce the person you want
c) make them fall in love with you.

(Sorry about the order, but that's the reality of how it usually happens!) Most people accept there are a few underlying musts to this formula – few would argue looking healthy, dressing well, and being generally pleasant helps. But not too many people stop to think about their body language. Which is odd (not to mention rather stupid), when 55 per cent of the impression we have of someone is based on their body language.

So why should you believe in the power of body language?
This is a good point in the book to reiterate where all the information you've been reading ultimately came from. So far, you're (hopefully) faithfully pointing your toes, steepling fingers, and doing God knows what else. But it's around this point that it all starts to get a bit hard and people think: "Ummm… exactly why am I doing all this again? Like, how did zoologists and body language experts come up with all this seeming nonsense about keeping your palms up, wrists flashed, and chin dipped?"

Well, by studying animals and humans and watching how both act in, and react to, different situations. From there, they're able to piece together common body language gestures for different moods (happy, hostile) and personality types (introvert, confident). If all the confident people they studied, stood with their right finger in their ear, that gesture then goes on the "confident person" list. (Tell me you know I'm joking about the finger in the ear!)

Experiment with body language, and ask friends if you're being **too obvious or too subtle?**

Now, this is how it works to help you: if you stand, sit, walk, and generally do whatever other confident/sexy/attractive/ successful/popular people do, people will think you are also confident (sexy, etc.) because that's what's proved true in the past. You'll also find that as you adopt the gestures of a confident person, others around will react to you differently, which in turn will help to give you greater confidence.

So even if some of this advice does sound a bit weird and you aren't really sure why putting your thumbs on display is going to get you laid, trust me. Hang in there. This is a quick, visual reference book so I've spared you lots of the theory but all the tips are tried and tested and come from reputable sources.

Mixed messages

Struggling to read someone's body language? Try this:

- **Check their signals:** take a step back to observe properly.
- **Count to four:** can you see at least four signs that they like you? Wishful thinking makes us read too much into others' body language.
- **Change position:** if they mirror you, it's good news.
- **Leave briefly, then come back:** if they're still in the same place, they were hoping you'd return to them.

Never judge on one thing alone. Always look for consistent messages.

Test their intentions by doing the following:

- **Step in, then back** While you're chatting, take a step forward into the space between you, then quickly step back again. This draws attention to the space between you. If they're keen, they'll now step forward to close the gap without really knowing why.

- **Drop your voice so it's almost a whisper** If they stand where they are, cup their ear, and shout "I can't hear you. Can you speak up?", they aren't interested in getting close.

How to touch

He needs to be careful

Touch is vital but when, where, and how someone touches is critical. Because men are more sex-driven than women, and women have more body parts that have sexual connotations (breasts, thighs, bottom), men need to avoid any erotic zone, or risk being branded "he's only after me for sex".

She doesn't

Because women tend to be driven by romance, touches on his personal parts (bar *that* part) are seen as innocent. She can place a hand on his chest, to show she shares his feelings, or even his thigh – though the closer her hand is to his genitals, the more likely it is to be taken as a come-on.

No-go zones

Men are physically stronger than women. Which means any of his gestures that involve touching taboo areas, coming too close, or gripping can feel threatening. It also pays to keep it soft and light. We touch the way we like to be touched and men's skin is tougher, meaning their touch is harder.

Much better

By stepping back, loosening the grip, and adding an "I won't harm you" smile, the first gesture (*bottom left*) will be received as it was intended: to reassure, rather than inspire fear. In the same way, moving his hand from the top of her bottom to the middle of her back turns a fondling gesture into a guiding one.

Arm clasped behind back. It's a "get hold of yourself" gesture. Men, particularly, stand this way if it's crucial to maintain self-control.

Rocking
New mothers instinctively rock babies to soothe them, at the same speed as the heartbeat heard in the womb. As adults, we recreate this security by rocking on our heels.

Subtle signs

Some body language looks so bad, it's obviously never a good idea to use it. But it's the seemingly insignificant gestures that can often make or break that date.

Displacement activities Simply avoiding things like tightly folded arms won't keep you out of trouble. More subtle actions – like those opposite – will also strongly influence who's still hanging around when you come back from getting a drink, and who hot-footed it the second your back was turned. Some of our less lovable habits are

Under pressure **our true feelings "leak out"** in gestures.

called displacement activities: small, trivial, repetitive, fidgety things we do when under stress. I'm talking drumming fingers, tapping feet, jiggling legs, clicking pens, shredding napkins, doodling, checking and rechecking schedules, and the dozens of other movements people make when under stress that annoy the hell out of everyone else. If people seem agitated, uncomfortable, or don't seem to relax around you, watch for any constant fiddles and fidgets.

The body rarely lies We often play with any ring signifying commitment when we talk to someone who's both forbidden and gorgeous. It subconsciously rids us of commitment for that stolen period. Naughty? Yes. But it's not your fault if it's automatic, is it now?

Instant turn-ons

Our eyes can respond to one and a half million simultaneous messages – hardly surprising, then, that we use them to communicate more than any other part of our body. This is one reason why big eyes are a plus – the signals are clearer. Make yours look huge by doing what Princess Di did whenever a camera pointed her way: dip your chin so the top of your face, including your eyes, seems bigger. You can also try:

- **An eye flash** If a man is looking at a woman and their eyes lock, she will often raise her upper eyelids slightly and rapidly. It's a subtle eye-opening movement which says to him, "Yes, it is definitely you I'm looking at".

- **Can't take my eyes off you** When we're attracted, we really do have difficulty dragging our eyes away. The person stops talking, someone else starts – and we're still gazing adoringly even though they're silent. Do it deliberately for startling effect. Keep your eyes on theirs for a slow count of five during the silence that follows after you, or they, stop talking.

- **Fake "bedroom eyes"** These are essentially eyes with big pupils (they dilate when they like what they see) and lots of moisture (tears pool when we're excited by someone). Get the look by holding your eyes open extra-wide, trying not to blink until tears form, then shutting them for a few seconds to block out light (another way to alter pupil size). When you reopen, voilà! You'll have shiny eyes with lots of pupil action!

Dip
your chin
**and do
a Di.**

If in doubt, smile! A simple smile, when we don't expose any teeth and our lips simply curve upwards, is very effective. It's also the right smile to use to signal sexual interest. A broad smile removes all mystery, making "the chase" redundant and you appear friendly rather than flirty. This is not necessarily a good thing!

To pout or not to pout? Marilyn Monroe mastered it, the rest of us can end up looking like a rather sad extra in a porn film. But lasciviously licking the lips and pouting both draw attention to the mouth, home of many sexual pleasures. It also highlights the fact that a female's lips are more luscious than a man's. When aroused, female lips (both kinds) become swollen and redder in colour – hence why a pout and lipstick are seen as sexy. Pouting makes lips seem fuller; it also explains why bright red lipstick is seen as so blatantly sexy – it's brash.

A slow and secretive smile is the sexiest.

I spy… a party animal When we do things we shouldn't, our body often finds a way to tell us something is wrong. An eye twitch is a muscle contraction or spasm usually brought on by tension or stress (working too hard, or drinking, smoking, partying etc. too much). If it's you twitching away, ease up and get some sleep. If it's the person chatting you up, they might be the party animal – or be feeling under pressure. Ditto the person who is blinking excessively – they're nervous or insecure.

Sense your type

Around 55 per cent of us "see" the world, 15 per cent "hear" it, and 30 per cent "feel" it.

How we filter the constant stream of information we receive about the world depends on which of our senses is the most dominant. You might both be in the same restaurant on a first date, but what you're experiencing could be dramatically different. Visuals are looking at the décor, what everyone's wearing, and admiring the food presentation. Auditory people are busy eavesdropping, listening to the background music, and reading the menu out loud. Kinesthetics (or kinos) feel the world, so are driven by physical sensation. They're the ones touching the tablecloth, drinking in the atmosphere, and trying to analyse your emotions. When we "click" with someone it usually means they're the same type – they've travelled through the world taking the same journey.

Who's who? We all experience the world through sight, sound, and feelings so most of us are a mix of all three types. But post-childhood, nearly all of us have one sense that is our favourite and becomes dominant. It's in your interest to know which type your lusted-after love object prefers, because if you know how they relate to the world, you can communicate to them on their wavelength.

When you match yourself up with another person's favourite sense, you're not only talking the same language, but seeing through the same eyes, hearing through the same ears, and feeling the same feelings. How could they not be seduced by you?

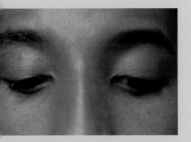

1

Eyes down = kinesthetic

They look to their hearts. Not surprisingly, they're big touchers, often physical, and highly sexed!

Tips: Buy presents with textures that feel nice to stroke, talk slowly – it takes longer to feel words than see or hear them.

2

Eyes to the side = auditory

They look to their ears. Things need to sound good to get their attention. They've got great voices and often work with words and sounds in music or broadcasting.

Tips: Take them to concerts, leave voicemail, and instigate long chats.

3

Eyes up = visuals

They look to their imaginations. Because they "see" the world, visuals care about how things look. They talk fast and move their hands a lot, drawing pictures with words.

Tips: Look good, take them to pretty places, and use phrases like "I see".

Sexual signals

Having naughty thoughts often leads to auto-erotic touching – this means subconsciously touching ourselves. There are three (very good) reasons why we do this:

- **The first** is to draw attention to a body part we'd like the other person to notice – the reason why females slide hands over thighs, waists, hips, and upper arms, and both sexes stroke their lips with their fingers (sometimes even slipping one sexily inside the mouth).

- **We also touch ourselves to tease** – "Wouldn't you like me to be touching you like this? Or you touching me?"

- **Finally, we touch because it feels good** When we become sexually excited, blood rushes to our extremities (no, not just that one!), engorging the lips and making them feel supersensitive. If the person you're with starts drinking or eating faster when you flirt with them, it's having the right effect.

Get close

Gauge your date's response by leaning forward lots, while keeping your feet back in the intimate zone. Then touch in a safe place (lower arm or hand). If they don't withdraw, it's safe to slide into the snuggle zone.

Think sex and you'll probably touch your mouth.

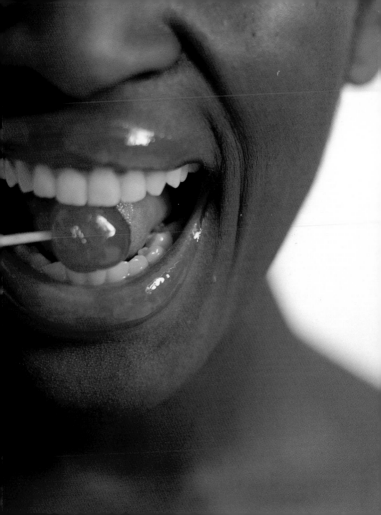

Touch and tease

If we'd like to sleep with someone, we often instinctively kiss, lick, or caress objects… Especially those that subconsciously remind us of sex.

Women suck pens and fingers (pretend penises), lick ice-creams, and let spoons slide sensually out of their mouth (pretend oral sex). Yes, sometimes it's unintentional and meaningless, but combined with other positive signs, pseudo-sexual signals count. Particularly watch if they start playing with their wine glass. Women slide fingers up and down the stem, men tend to circle the rim with their finger – cleverly

> # Sticking something in your mouth can be a sign that you're up for it.

reflecting the different way we touch respective body parts! She'll use her hair to show she's keen. Once she's got your attention, she'll signal availability by running her fingers through her hair, fluffing it, or (best of all) doing a head toss so it flicks and bounces around. It's designed to show how healthy (and therefore young) her hair (and she) is.

Watch for men stroking their ties (some say an arrow pointing to the penis), fiddling with change in their pocket (the closest he can get to a quick fiddle without getting arrested), sliding rings up and down a finger (imitating thrusting), or rubbing their nose (a phallic symbol).

Standing signals

If you want some insider info on your date, just check out the way they're standing.

Straddled, feet wide apart
The guy who stands with feet apart has a flashing sign above his head saying, "Pick me if you want a real man". Dominant men stand like this because it widens their body and makes them take up lots of space.

Legs loosely crossed at the calves (*left*) is a protective standing position but isn't hostile. This person is just nervous and uncomfortable – less flirting, more friendly, reassuring chat.

Legs crossed like blades of scissors A favourite for those who are submissive and shy. They're all yours to bring out of their shell though – the position means they couldn't leave quickly even if they wanted to.

Sneaky tricks

Want someone's attention in a crowd? Then just whisper to the person next to you. It sounds odd, but works like magic! Make direct eye contact with them, give a little smile, then whisper into the ear of the person you're with. It doesn't matter what you say – they'll still think you're talking about them and curiosity drives most of us nuts.

Even if they're shy, they'll keep stealing glances in your direction. If they're confident, they'll find a way to stand close, raising a quizzical eyebrow. The brave will come straight up and ask what you said. Whispers make us think someone is saying something awfully nice or awfully horrible about us – why else would they whisper it? Either way, it gets the adrenalin pumping and them looking your way. (Pretty easy from there to convince them it's complimentary!)

Put your coat on top of theirs. **Are they pleased or panicked** to see your things muddled?

Whispers also work when you're already chatting to the person. Once you've both warmed up, lean forwards, and whisper into their ear. It could be conspiratorial ("I don't know about you, but I'm not convinced about that painting") or a compliment ("You're very funny by the way"). Then simply pull back, smile, and continue the conversation.

How to reel them in

Okay, so we've covered most of the body language basics. Are you feeling confident? Great! Now try these really devious ploys to grab their attention and win them over:

- **Walk tall** As you approach look ahead, not down, and square your shoulders. Walk with an even pace with a slight bounce, tilt your pelvis forwards, hold your head high, half smile, and look at other people. You'll feel more involved in the world by seeing what's going on around you, not to mention look more confident. All will get you noticed and to first base!

- **Make up a (flattering) nickname** It makes them feel special because it means you've noticed something unusual about them. It also instantly puts things on a more personal level, the same effect as remembering to mention their name.

- **Ask for a headache pill** If he's out to impress, he'll search high and low to find you one, then has the perfect excuse to hang around and look after you. If you're feeling really cheeky and confident, try asking him to massage your hands or head – it really does help ease tension and creates a nice little excuse for some sensual touching.

- **Ask for a light** If they hand you a lighter, they're shy, not interested or seeing someone else. If they offer to light your cigarette for you and lean in, up the intensity by making direct eye contact as the flame connects.

- **Sit next to them** Even better if you can make a bit of fuss to do so. (Do it in a friendly way and you won't look desperate.) Do they look pleased? Snuggle in? Or move their body or an object to create distance between you? Moving elsewhere should be obvious (i.e. the "then he-said, then I said" phone call won't be necessary later that night).

- **Play mum** Everyone likes being taken care of – particularly if the person coming to their aid happens to be captivatingly sexy! To "mother" them, notice when they need things (a fresh drink, fresh air, a jacket, the time…).

- **Play it personal** If you want to move things beyond boring chit-chat, volunteer something personal about yourself. The more you open up, the more likely they are to follow.

- **Be happy** Unless you've got the self-deprecating humour routine down to pat, few of us get away with being constantly grumpy. Who would you rather hang around with? A depressed, unhappy moaner or a funny optimistic, who makes life seem bright and full of promise?

The giveaway sign they fancy you

Glance over your shoulder when you visit the bathroom during those first few meetings and it's almost guaranteed you'll know if they're sexually interested or not. If you see them checking out your bottom, it's nearly always a yes – for both sexes. Peer around the corner to see what they do next: after you've disappear from sight, their next move is usually to check their hair is behaving.

Symbolic stripping

Body language is both primitive and logical. If someone's pushing the right buttons, it tries very hard to get us naked with that person.

This is why we undo buttons, loosen ties, and push up our sleeves – we're symbolically stripping. It's the polite, public version of slipping into something "more comfortable" (easily removable) and it sends LOUD sexual signals. A woman who lets a strap fall off her shoulder – and leaves it there – is saying, "Look, I'm getting undressed already". Leaving a shoulder exposed allows him to imagine she is already topless. Semi-clothed is often sexier than completely naked, which is why both sexes wear "peekaboo" clothes – ripped jeans or tops and (for her) skirts with splits – all serving up a tantalizing glimpse of flesh.

We often start undressing
without even realizing it.

What they do with their coat If they unbutton their jacket, it's a sign they're opening themselves up to meet people. Men stand with hands on both hips to ensure they take up lots of room and look bigger; women hold their arms close to their sides to achieve the opposite. If she leans forwards and brings her arms in close to her body so the breasts press together and cleavage deepens, you really can turn back the bedsheets!

How to open them up

There's always a certain tension in the air when you first meet someone you like, and it's good to know how to lighten the mood. So if you think they're sex-on-legs but the cloud hovering above them means you don't stand a chance, simply change their mood or mind, by changing their position.

1

Mirror them
This is the only time I'll encourage you to mirror bad body language! Cross whatever they've got crossed and stand the way they are to subliminally show you're on the same emotional level.

2

Unfold one arm
Once you've warmed them up with words, subtly drop one arm. If, after a while, they haven't dropped one of theirs, cross both arms again, keep the conversation non-threatening, and smile, before trying this tactic again.

3

Wait for them to follow

If they're trusting you, they'll start to physically/emotionally open up. Even if arms are crossed but loosened, it's a start. If nothing's happening, hand them something to force them to break the hold.

4

Drop both arms

You've now led by example and shifted your posture from closed to open, one step at a time. Be patient at this point. Dropping their second arm – the final barrier between you – is maybe a bit scary!

5

Don't make any sudden moves

They've now completely exposed themselves (so to speak) but now's not the time for big gestures like moving too close or touching. Stay friendly but not flirty for at least 10 minutes (and that does mean not so much as a hair-flick!).

Being a **sex kitten**

A revealing dress in a bright colour and most men would lay bets she's broadcasting sexual availability. What's more likely is that she's attracting the attention of the bunch, with the hope of finding one mate.

Bare thighs Exposing the upper thigh says "Come here big boy" clearer than any words could ever express.

Being **subtly sexy**

High collar = class
Despite her breasts being accentuated by this sweater, any top higher than the neckline sends schoolmarmish signals. The most over-the-top flirting moves are fine when dressed conservatively.

The demure arm In this posture there's a subtle change in arm position. By placing it along one thigh, she's covering herself. Holding it back and away from the body (left) invites admirers to take a good, uninterrupted look at her.

Take a few risks, and see what happens.

Tracey's top tips

Leave a lasting impression

Don't ruin a great entrance by blowing it on departure and making a fuss about leaving. Insist on saying loud goodbyes to everyone and you'll look insecure and desperate to be included next time. Whatever you do, don't look back when walking out. If people are watching you exit, they'll admire you even more if you don't glance back anxiously.

Colour people's perceptions

The colour you wear and where you wear it are all highly significant. A siren red sweater worn under a suit to a business function suggests confidence and power, a red miniskirt worn to meet your partner's parents suggests stupidity.

Don't forget to move

Confident people change positions once every two or three minutes, altering their weight and moving subtly and smoothly into new postures. The trick is to think energetically without moving too rapidly or fidgeting. (Easier than it sounds!)

It beats botox

Wage war on wrinkles the cheap, pain-free way: hang around someone adorable. When we look at someone we like, our faces relax, soften, and glow; harsh lines fade and we look younger. It works a treat long term too. When we're conscious of people watching our faces, we adjust our expressions to look "perky". But before long they soon fall into the facial position we assume most of the time. If you're mostly happy, that won't be a problem, will it?

the**date**

If you think dating is difficult these days, just cast your mind back. The "love letter" – the text or email – is certainly a lot less hassle than the old variety.

How it used to be If you think waiting for a phone call is bad, imagine lying around your castle, agonising about does she/he like me for days or weeks on end before the mounted messenger finally arrived! Today's equivalent – texts and emails – offers cheap, immediate communication. We're able to tell the person we lust after exactly how we feel, at the exact moment we feel it. Fabulous, eh? Or not…

Text regret Just about all of us have woken up after a heavy night and nearly passed out when our mobile phone swims into view, looking suspiciously used. What felt right to send at 3am – drunk, emotional, and desperate for a cuddle (etc.) – suddenly seems completely inappropriate at 7am. And you can bet your next five headache pills, it was. The main plus of texts and email – instant gratification – is also the main negative. Emotions like love, lust, anger, and jealousy can be fleeting but they're powerful and have a tendency to take

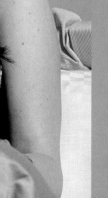

over and hold other more sensible brain inhabitants – like logic and judgement – hostage. Overcome by overwhelming emotion, plenty of us reach for our mobile phone to express by text – only to lose the respect of existing and potential lovers by misjudging the situation.

How to make sure it doesn't happen to you Never ever send an angry, exceedingly soppy, needy, or emotional text after two drinks and don't text *anyone* after three drinks (bar your mother, best friend or long, long, long-term partner – and even then only to make arrangements or to be exceedingly nice). A few other things:

Don't assume someone's not interested because they don't answer a text or email. Mobiles get lost, stolen, and broken. Technology isn't infallible and not everyone carries their phone wherever they go or checks their emails every hour. So if they don't answer immediately, don't assume you've upset them or that they don't feel the same way.

Be careful with humour and innuendo Delivered at the right time, in the right tone, and with a sardonic raise of an eyebrow, that wicked one-liner about the nun and the condom might well have them holding their sides with laughter. Sadly, some – actually scratch that, most – humour doesn't translate to text and only a fraction survives email. Avoid saying anything which could be taken the wrong way. In person, it's easy to tell if you've just accidentally offended someone – and to fix it before things get into a horrible mess. A misconstrued text or email can set off a horrid chain reaction. Save important topics for when you're together.

The blind email date Flirting via email with someone you've never set eyes on is both irresistibly appealing and ridiculously stupid. Exactly the reason why we all do it! You start out being a bit playful with someone you deal with through work, next minute, there you are about to meet them for the first time and practically passing out with anticipation. Sometimes, it's lust at first look. More often, it's mutual and massive disappointment: what worked through words, doesn't cut it in the flesh. Pained, polite emails replace the previously frisky ones – besides, you're too busy sending flirtatious messages to the new person in the overseas office who sounds soooo sexy. So by all means go for it but be warned!

If you start to argue, call rather than text – talking **fixes it** faster.

Warning: text messaging can be addictive Lots of people – men particularly – find it easier to express their true feelings via text and email because it's not face to face (hence it is a lot less embarrassing). Men also like this type of communication because they're often not as "in touch" with their feelings as women, so spur-of-the-moment, face-to-face relationship chats render them speechless. With the written word, they get time to think about what they really want to say and how to say it. All great practice but easy to hide behind. My advice: use text messaging to enhance your real-life relationship, not as a substitute.

Hand signals

Face propped up

This classic boredom pose, with an elbow resting on the table, is bad news! If this is you, be aware your date is expecting you to yawn next. If it's them, rethink just how funny the story about Aunt Marge's cupcakes really is. Leap into damage control: lean forward, touch their forearm, and move onto everyone's favourite topic – themselves.

Arm crossed, hand over mouth

Crossing an arm in front of you effectively shuts people out. And we put our hands in front of our mouth to subliminally stop words we shouldn't say coming out. We also do it when we whisper something we don't want others to lip-read. It is associated with being rude and secretive. Never a good look, least of all on a date.

Hands loosely clasped, on table

This is the way I get people on a date to sit if they're nervous. It's not ideal because your arms are still crossed, but it's way better than the alternative – folding your arms or clasping your fingers together (both signs you're touchy or terrified). By sitting this way, you're getting comfort without looking tense by holding your own hand.

Hands to chest

Holding your hands to your chest briefly will make you look animated and honest. We do it to pledge loyalty and allegiance. If a guy sits like this, he wants you to know he's genuine. If a girl does it, it's a signal she's open. But if her hands fly quickly to her chest, it could mean you've shocked or surprised her and she's being protective.

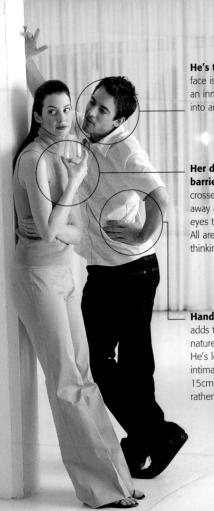

He's talking at her His face is too close, turning an innocent conversation into an attack.

Her drink forms a barrier With one arm crossed, she's looking away and raising her eyes to the heavens. All are signs that she's thinking "Help!".

Hand on hip This adds to the aggressive nature of this pose. He's leaning into her intimate zone (within 15cm) and harassing rather than seducing.

Spot who's hard work

I'm all for fresh starts and second chances, but it's always better to know what you're letting yourself in for. If you see clusters of the following body language, chances are that the person's sporting a few emotional bruises, which could spell trouble:

- **Too much eye contact:** aggressive and expecting trouble.
- **Refusing to meet your eyes:** hiding something or cripplingly shy.
- **"Blank" eyes:** they've emotionally shut down.
- **Suppressing or hiding smiles:** could be haunted by a tragedy (or they hate their teeth!).
- **Rubbing their hand on their forehead when they speak:** they have the troubles of the world on their shoulders.
- **Laughing at the end of a sentence:** insecure, discrediting what they've just said.
- **Rocking or swaying:** they want to run away.
- **Smiling, nodding too much:** too eager to please.
- **Over-mirroring body language:** desperate to be liked.
- **Over-exaggerated gestures:** pumped full of self-importance.
- **Self-touch:** usually means they're self-obsessed.

Who really sounds trustworthy? Listen to how someone speaks. If they consider you their equal, the volume of their voice will be neither high nor low. Too loud and they're dominating, too low shrieks submissive. A harsh, ragged voice grates and repels, a too-smooth talker will make you feel suspicious (Am I being conned?). Ditto fast-talkers. The saying "fast talker" – meaning untrustworthy – is steeped in truth. We do talk faster when we're trying to dig ourselves out of a hole.

Mid-date checklist

Halfway through the date, escape to the loo. Take some time out to objectively review what's happening with both of you. Believe me, it will pay off enormously. You've had time to get to know each other a little but you're not so drunk your judgement's impaired! Ask yourself the following:

What are they saying? Ideally, the conversation will flow freely and meander in all sorts of directions as you gently probe and get to know each other. Sticking with small talk won't get you anywhere but neither will instantly diving in: if you're trading intimate secrets before the main course it's going way too fast. Aim for the odd shared intimacy and don't reveal another until they've done the same. First-date secrets should be served like ping-pong balls – traded one for one.

What's their body language telling me? Look for at least four signs saying the same thing (this is known as "The Rule of Four" – see page 8), then add a huge dollop of common sense. Consider where you are – we behave differently in different circumstances. If the restaurant is formal, the date probably will be. If it's relaxed and laid back but they're behaving like they're having tea with the Queen, they're self-conscious and need relaxing. Don't jump to conclusions. If your date didn't smile back when you smiled on the way back from the loo, they're not arrogant, they're just blind without glasses and too vain to wear them with you. Most importantly, watch for changes in body language. On a great date, the person should be moving closer, making more eye contact, and sneakily checking you out. Even uncrossing their arms and/or feet and looking at you more is a step in the right direction.

What signals am I sending them? As part of your mid-date review, it's important to check your own body language – is it clear, positive, and an appropriate response to theirs? If you're unsure if your date likes you as a friend or lover, introduce touch. Lean over to touch their hand, forearm, or shoulder. If they like you and aren't shy, they'll touch you back within ten minutes or so. Later, touch them lightly on their lower back (to shift them out the way or guide them). Do they jump away from your touch or arch their back and move into it, looking over their shoulder to smile at you? It's recommended that you touch three times, for three seconds each time, on a first date.

If you want someone to open up to you, simply open up to them a little.

Do I want to move things on? Think objectively about what you now know about this person given the benefit of time. Are they fitting into your previous perception of them or turning out to be even better than you'd thought? Fantastic! Let it move forwards. If you think that you're getting mixed signals, consider going on somewhere else. The quickest way to change someone's attitude is to change their position by getting them to move. See if this offers a better glimpse into their personality. It could be that the environment you were in was making them feel uncomfortable or that they just felt "stuck".

The dinner date

Going for dinner together means sitting opposite each other, separated only by a table. Women handle this well (lots of coffees with girlfriends), shy men find it acutely embarrassing. It's face-to-face and it's intimate, so how *are* you supposed to sit?

Direct gaze and animated face Everything about this girl's pose (*right*) says, "You have my full attention and I want to hear what you have to say". In action, you'd see that her blink rate is slow; the more anxious someone is, the more often they blink.

> **Anxious hands** play with objects or **hang onto each other** for reassurance.

Hands on table, palms up You score big points for placing your hands on the table. If you let them fall naturally, chances are they'll land uncrossed with palms up. This is good – it says, "I have nothing to hide". Even if they're shaking like a leaf, it's better to have them in view than sitting on them or shoving them between your thighs.

Closed posture Clenched hands, tense posture, and downward glances give an impression of being "folded in" – not open to your date (or a relationship). Sadly, it's more likely to be due to nerves and the person is probably unaware of the signals they're sending.

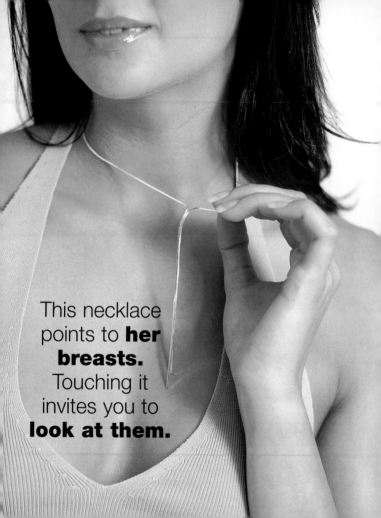

Flirting props

For an accurate assessment of what your date's really feeling, look beyond what's being said to check out the following:

What's happening with their drink?
- **It's good** if her fingers are stroking up and down the stem or outside of the glass or his finger is rubbing the rim. (Both are imitating how you'd like to touch each other's bits.) If she's sucking or nibbling her straw while making direct eye contact, make a move.
- **It's bad** if they're holding their drink chest height or higher as this is a barrier. If they don't drop it in a few minutes, give up. If they drop it but then wrap both hands around the glass, still give up.

What are they doing with their hair?
- **It's good** if she removes her hair from behind her ears and shakes it loose – she's relaxing and in play mode. If he touches, musses, or smooths his hair, he's preening to look good for you.
- **It's bad** if she pushes her hair behind her ears – she means business. Repeatedly smoothing his hair means he's nervous.

How much space is there between you and your date?
- **It's good** if there's hardly any.
- **It's bad** if there's loads.

What fills the space?
- **It's good** if there's nothing. They've moved objects to clear the way.
- **It's bad** if they've erected a wall. If she's placed her bag, drink, and jacket between you she might as well be wearing an asbestos suit.

Clothes and colours

What you wear says a lot about who you are. Dress "sexily" –
anything plunging, curve-clinging, or thigh-skimming for her; tight,
chest-revealing, or suspiciously thought-about for him – and people
will assume you're on the pull. Which you probably are!

The colour you wear on a date also speaks its own language
to the person you're with.
- **Black:** I'm fashionable, stylish, and creative.
- **Red:** I'm happy to be the centre of attention and unafraid of
  showing my emotions.
- **Hot pink:** I want to stand out from the crowd.
- **Baby pink:** Treat me gently.
- **Dark blue:** I mean business.
- **Light or mid-blue:** I'm calm and focused.
- **Beige:** I'm a little unsure of myself.
- **White:** Notice me, not my clothes.
- **All-white on men:** I'm over 50 and to be avoided.

Glasses and sunglasses

When and how people wear and remove their glasses offers
a plethora of clues. If someone takes them off, cleans them
slowly, then puts them back on they are probably stalling for time.
If someone breathes on the lenses and polishes them, it's a sign
that they want a clear view of the world. If you keep removing and
replacing your glasses, you may be seen as indecisive. Take them
off while revealing personal information, and you let someone in.
Sucking on the ends of glasses means you're either seeking
comfort – or sex!

Making eyes

We use our eyes to assess and express – to work out how a lover is feeling and to express how we are feeling.

The role eyes play in couple connection is extraordinary.
They're nicknamed "the gateway to love" for good reason: eye contact directly influences whether we'll fall in love with someone or not. The more we like someone, the longer we lock eyes with them and the more likely the brain is to produce PEA (phenylethylamine) – a substance released when we fall in love.

> # The trick to flirting is to make **the eyes** look larger without staring.

The more PEA floating around your system, the more likely you are to fall in love with someone. Locking eyes into a mutual lover's gaze – where we unconsciously read pupil dilations (deep black pools mean all is well, tiny pinprick pupils make us feel uneasy) – isn't the only thing you can do to make your date fall for you. Try any (or all) of the following:

Wide eyes Pulling back our eyelids makes our eyes look bigger, giving an affect of innocent attentiveness. Animal and human babies have big eyes in proportion to their face and few people can resist feeling protective or nurturing of them. As adults we still feel protective when we see someone with large eyes. Widening the eyes into "look after me" works for both sexes.

Smiling eyes Think about something that makes you happy and your eyes will sparkle and dance. Instead of always smiling at a potential lover by moving your mouth into a broad smile, smile with your eyes instead. Research shows the more you use your eyes to send messages, the more responsive people will be to you.

The greater the pupil dilation the greater the love.

Wandering eyes Being "eyeballed" – given the once-over – by some sleaze in a bar is an enormous turn-off. Feeling a much-fancied date's eyes travel lustily over your body on a deliberate but tasteful visual journey, is quite another thing. Once it's clear the two of you want more than just companionship, it's okay to let your eyes wander.

Point to your eyes Eyes follow moving things, so use your fingers (or a pen) to lift their eyes to yours. Once they're there, hold them with a five-second burst of intense gazing.

Lustful eyes Think Marilyn Monroe – lowered eyelids and raised eyebrows, mouth half-open. She effectively reproduced the expression that appears on people's faces just before they orgasm. Doing it hints at what's in store later.

Why candlelit dinners work Our pupils dilate when we look at something we like or love – consequently, we're instinctively attracted to large pupils. Italian women in the 18th century put tiny drops of belladonna (an extract from the deadly nightshade plant) into their eyes to artificially dilate their pupils. Luckily, less drastic measures work equally as well. A good old-fashioned candlelit dinner doesn't just soften our faces, showing off our looks to best effect, it shows off our pupil dilation as well. The less light, the bigger the pupil.

Can you scientifically measure love? Psychologist Zick Rubin found couples in love look at each other 75 per cent of the time when talking. In normal conversation, we look at someone for between 30 and 60 per cent. Use it to up the chances of your date falling in love with you by looking at them for 75 per cent of the time. Their brain realizes the last time someone looked at them that long in one stretch it meant they were in love, so it assumes they're in love with you as well.

And, finally, look for these signs:
- **Shiny, glistening eyes:** the person is excited and could be in love. When we feel emotional, tear production increases slightly. This gives the eye surface a glistening quality.
- **Rapid blinking:** the normal blink rate is 15–20 blinks per minute (women blink more than men), but it can increase to four or five times that when we feel under pressure. We blink more when we're tired, anxious, stressed, or excited.
- **Face watching:** when we like someone, we tend to check their facial expressions to reassure us that they're as happy as we want them to be.

Listen up

Listening is as much a skill as talking. As the saying goes, you've got two ears and one mouth – use them in proportion! It's sometimes more important to know when not to say something than it is to say the right thing.

Women and men listen in different ways Women do what's called "active listening" – throw in lots of nods, smiles, and "uhuhs"; men think if they say anything at all, it'll be seen as interrupting. Because of this, each sex often mistakenly assumes lack of interest.

> It's **as important** to know when **not to say something** than it is to say the right thing.

Listen out for danger signs Keep your ears open at the beginning of a relationship to check the person is all they say they are. These are clues they're covering something up:

- **Verbal distancing:** Liars use "I", "me", or "mine" less in an attempt to emotionally distance themselves. "The match was great" rather than, "I enjoyed the match".
- **You won't believe this, but...** Well aware of how dodgy it all sounds, they figure if they acknowledge it rather than pretend it's all perfectly plausible, you might just fall for it.
- **Answering a question with a question:** They're buying time.

Mismatched

Mismatched facial expressions If they'd "clicked", it's likely they'd look at each other, or in the same direction.

Hand on her chin . There's no "rhythm" between their body parts to suggest they think the same.

Postural conflict Are their feet deliberately mismatched? If someone refuses to mirror, they are trying to be seen as different or superior.

Matched

It means more if he mirrors you Generally, men are less likely than women to mirror or "echo" because they're less concerned with being liked.

Emotional matching If they mirror each other – doing the same things at the same time – it's a sign they're on the same emotional wavelength.

Postural matching Mirroring works two ways: the stronger the "click", the more you do it; and the more you do it, the stronger the connection becomes.

Hand-holding clues

Hold hands to find out how someone feels about you. The person whose thumb lands on top, is usually in the power position (in the image, *bottom left*, it's the girl).

The direction of the palm is also telling. If they turn your hand so their palm faces back (like the man in the main picture, *opposite*), they're in the front, control position. A kinder interpretation is they're being protective, but be warned! Test which is which by twisting your hand so that yours is "in front". If they quickly turn it back again, they're intent on being boss.

Linked fingers (*bottom left*) mean they want to mesh every body part. It's much more significant than the simple palm-to-palm clasp (*bottom right*), the trademark of a settled couple, showing affection and acceptance. Why? It's much harder to break the hold and usually means you've got a firm grip on each other and are reluctant to let go. The couple who "grip" don't tend to let anything come between them.

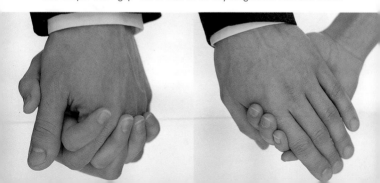

The palm direction says this man is the **boss of the relationship.**

Space games

People are territorial. If they don't like you, they won't want your things on their side of the table!

Start playing with an object
Make sure it's on "your" side. Then surreptitiously push it to their side and take your hands away.

Watch how they react
If they're not keen, they'll instinctively push it back to your side – sensing you're trying to get close without really knowing why. But if they leave or hold the object, it's likely they want to rev things up.

Or try this...
With your forearms on the table, wrap your fingers around your glass and push it to their side. The person who fancies you will also lean forwards, and push *their* glass to your side of the table. If they lean back or do nothing, they're not interested.

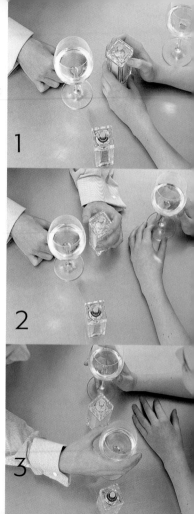

It's all in the kiss

According to legend, the French kiss was invented by medieval knights to find out if their wives had been secretly supping at the mead barrel while they were gone. Rather amusing when you consider few of us would pass the alcohol detection test now!

Most people need some Dutch courage to pucker up for the first time with someone special because they realize how tremendously significant that first kiss is. Mouths are almost as complex as eyes, and kissing is where all the sexual synergy starts. Kiss someone and you can tell how they feel about you romantically and sexually, how they're likely to be in bed, how they'll perform oral sex – and whether you're a good biological match.

Trust your first kiss It's like swapping a biological business card. Sebaceous glands in the mouth and corners of your lips release semiochemicals, designed to stimulate sexual excitement. These combine with your own unique saliva fingerprint and the end result is passed on during kissing. If canny old Mother Nature doesn't determine it to be a good genetic mix, the first kiss won't taste or smell right for either of you, and this will reduce the chances of things moving forward.

If the first kiss doesn't spark sexual fireworks, few people will pursue someone. It's perhaps for this reason that the drive to kiss appears to be innate – something we do instinctively. Over 90 per cent of all peoples on record kiss, with the world's most frequent kissers being Westerners and Hindus.

They want to kiss you if they:

- **Lick their lips** Both sexes lick their lips when faced with something arousing.
- **Keep touching their mouth** When turned on, our lips are engorged. This makes us conscious of them so we touch them.
- **Eat or drink suggestively** Eating an ice-cream, then licking fingers afterwards – they're trying to advertize their talents.
- **Put their head close to yours** This closeness is nearly always an invitation to kiss.
- **Look at you with head tilted** This means that they're already getting into position!

> # If they start to chew, drink, or smoke faster, **they want to kiss you**.

Was the kiss welcome? Start by brushing soft, relaxed lips lightly against theirs, mouth slightly open. You'll know immediately if they're interested. It's not good news if their lips clench shut, or if they involuntarily pull back, or their lips and mouth feel cool. Keep going if everything feels hot, they part their lips, and lean towards the kiss. If one hand comes up to cradle the back of your head, they're particularly keen. The more passionate they want the kiss to be, the further they'll part their lips. People kiss the way they'd like to be kissed. Kiss passively, let them take the lead, then all you need to do is simply imitate whatever they do.

In 90 minutes
you can work out
**what makes
someone
tick.**

Tracey's top tips

Don't turn up late for a date

Time is a powerful non-verbal communicator – the more important you are, the less you have of it. People of higher status keep people waiting, people of lower status don't dare to. It doesn't matter if the train was late, you couldn't find your keys, or a neighbour cornered you near the letterbox, the message you send if you're late on a date is: "This isn't important to me. I don't care as much as you do."

Psychologically strip

It's a what-you-see-isn't-necessarily-what-you-get technique. Once you've established a certain image on the date, peel back a layer to reveal a totally unexpected side to yourself. Ms. Innocence who turns out to be quite feisty. The career girl who turns out to be shy. We all like to think we know the "real" person, and hidden depth is attractive.

Look beneath the mask

If someone seems stiff and oddly false, keep them talking and watch for "microexpressions" – fleeting glimpses that give away how they're really feeling. Shy and unsure people do what's called "masking" – a false expression deliberately composed to disguise a (usually inappropriate) expression (fear, insecurity) behind it.

Get them to lie down

A picnic with both of you lying on a rug isn't just romantic and sexy, it's the best way to get someone to open up. We remember more and are more reflective because we're less inclined to move, leaving us more likely to concentrate and more responsive to new suggestions.

Index

Acknowledgements

I must start these acknowledgements with an apology to everyone I love in my life: sorry for ignoring you while I wrote this and thank you for always understanding why.

Thanks to everyone at Dorling Kindersley, especially Christopher Davis, Corinne Roberts, Deborah Wright, Hermione Ireland, Serena Stent, Liz Statham, Catherine Bell, Hannah Moore, Emma Forge and Carole Ash in the UK office. With special and enormous thanks to my editor, Peter Jones. In the US, Therese Burke, Bill Barry, Carl Raymond, Tom Korman, Cathy Sears and Rachel Kempster. Thanks also to Russell Sadur for his lovely photos and Nigel and Bev from XAB, who are such an utter pleasure to work with. Thanks too to Vicki McIvor, my loyal and lovely friend and agent. There really aren't words to thank you enough for everything you do to make my life easier.

Finally, but always most importantly, my family, without whom I would simply shrivel up and die!

The **best dates laugh lots, smile often,** and don't take themselves too seriously. **What are you waiting for?**